AUSTRALIAN LANDSCAPES

DESERTS & SAVANNAHS IN AUSTRALIA

RACHEL DIXON

First published 2018 by
Redback Publishing
PO Box 357 Frenchs Forest NSW 2086
Australia

ISBN 978-1-925630-89-3 (paperback)
ISBN 978-1-925630-20-6 (hardback)

Author: Rachel Dixon
Editor: Jane Hinchey
Original illustrations © Redback Publishing 2018
Originated by Redback Publishing
Printed and bound in China by Leo Paper

Acknowledgements:
Abbreviations: l—left, r—right, b—bottom, t—top, c—centre, m—middle
We would like to thank the following for permission to reproduce photographs:
p9 State Library VIC - Camel team with Afghan drivers Central Australia, (p10b Tandrew22, p12r Hesperian, p20b Eric Tan, p26m Benjamint444, p26m Mr A Stanley 05, p26l Kdliss, p27m Ko¤ínek Milan at wikimedia commons), p25m beartales.me, p31tl Public Domain, https://commons.wikimedia.org/w/index.php?curid=386228.

A catalogue record for this book is available from the National Library of Australia

Contents

Deserts and Savannahs 4
Deserts Around the World 4
Australian Aboriginal People of the Deserts and Savannahs 6
Early Settlers in the Deserts and Savannahs 8
Water in Australia's Deserts 10
Deserts and the Australian Economy 12
Cattle Industry 13
Australian Deserts and Environmental Sustainability 14
Plants and Animals in Australia's Deserts 15

Australia's Largest Deserts

1. Great Victoria Desert 16
2. Great Sandy Desert 18
3. Tanami Desert 20
4. Simpson Desert 22
5. Gibson Desert 24
6. Little Sandy Desert 25
7. Strzelecki Desert 26
8. Sturt Stony Desert 27
9. Tirari Desert 28
10. Pedirka Desert 29

Nullarbor Plain 30
Glossary, Index 32

Deserts and Savannahs

The immense desert areas of Australia used to be called its 'dead heart'. Today we realise that deserts and savannahs have complex ecosystems, with plants and animals that have adaptations enabling them to survive there and not in any other location. Deserts are now iconic symbols of Australia and are no longer dismissed as useless, empty wastelands.

What is a Desert?

Deserts are places with an annual rainfall below 250mm. They are not always hot, and night-time temperatures in some Australian deserts can drop below zero.

Savannahs

Not all desert areas are expanses of dry sand. In Australia, water is available if you know where to look for it. The semi-arid grasslands, or savannahs, support Australia's beef cattle industry. The savannahs merge into the dry desert and the borders of savannah regions can easily become very arid if the weather changes and there is not enough rainfall in any one year.

Explorers

Early explorers crossed the deserts as a way of proving that people could conquer nature. The expeditions of Burke and Wills in 1866 and of Ludwig Leichhardt in 1848 both ended in tragedy when the explorers died in the desert.

Explorers were also searching for land that could be settled and for overland routes that would allow people to travel between the colonies without having to sail around the coast.

Deserts Around the World

Subtropical Deserts

Australia's deserts are subtropical, which means they are in the same category as the Sahara and Kalahari Deserts in Africa, and the Mojave Desert in the USA. These deserts are hot and dry.

Polar Deserts

The cold polar deserts of the world are in Antarctica in the south and the Arctic in the north. Although these deserts are covered in ice, there is little or no liquid water available in these locations when the temperature falls well below freezing.

Coastal Deserts

Coastal deserts occur mostly on the western coasts of continents due to the prevailing cooler ocean currents. There is less evaporation into the air from a cool ocean, so winds blow dry air across the land and produce little rain. The result is that these regions are some of the most arid in the world, despite being next to an ocean of water. The Namib Desert in Africa is a coastal desert, as is the coastal section of the Great Sandy Desert in Western Australia.

Australia's Top Ten Deserts

The top ten Australian Deserts by size

1. Great Victoria Desert
2. Great Sandy Desert
3. Tanami Desert
4. Simpson Desert
5. Gibson Desert
6. Little Sandy Desert
7. Strzelecki Desert
8. Sturt Stony Desert
9. Tirari Desert
10. Pedirka Desert

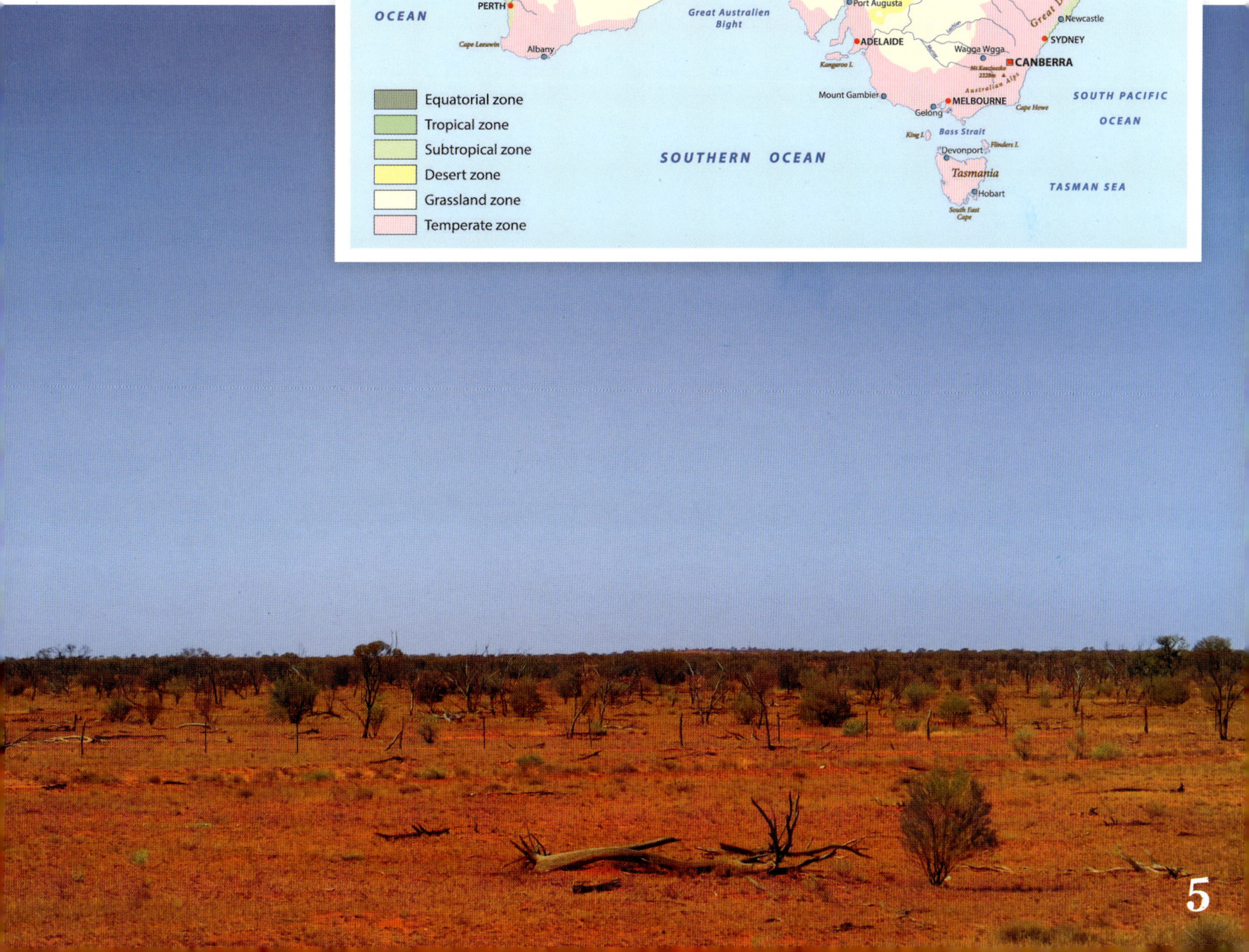

Australian Aboriginal People of the Deserts and Savannahs

Australian Aboriginal people of the deserts have lived there for thousands of years. Their methods of caring for the delicate desert and savannah ecosystems have allowed them to continue to survive in regions that have little water and sparse vegetation.

Traditional desert survival strategies

- Controlled burning during cooler weather encourages vegetation growth. It also reduces the occurrence of disastrous fires during the hotter months.
- A controlled, slow burn does not destroy all the animals in an area as it gives them time to move away. This use of fire is an important agricultural procedure to ensure a constant food supply.
- Small animals move into the burnt areas to feed on the new plant growth. The new food source leads to an increase in animal numbers, which makes hunting them easier. There is also less dense plant material for them to hide in.
- Water is managed by making maps of the water sources and maintaining a system of wells. These maps are still shared using art works and ceremonies, which show where water holes and springs are located and how long it takes to travel between them.

Traditional Bush Foods from the Desert

Plants

- quandongs
- yams
- bush tomatoes, plums, apples, raisins and limes
- lemon myrtle
- wattle and grass seeds which can be ground and baked

Insects

- grubs and caterpillars
- honey ants
- bee honey

Meat

- small mammals
- kangaroos and wallabies
- lizards and snakes
- birds

Ancestor creation spirits have entrusted Australian Aboriginal people with the deserts and given them a responsibility to care for the land and its animals for future generations of people. Landmarks across Australia's deserts have great spiritual significance and should be treated respectfully by visitors.

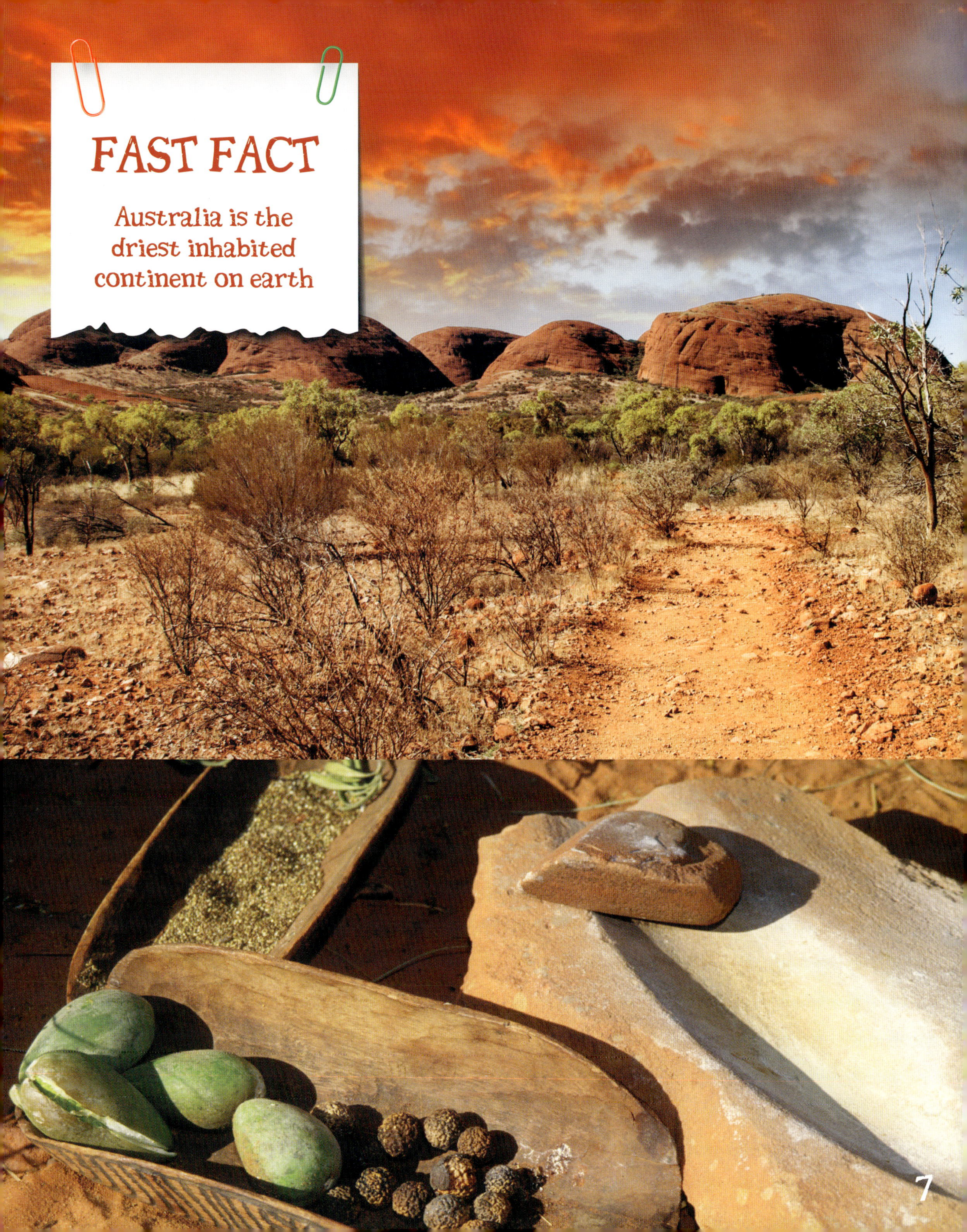
FAST FACT
Australia is the driest inhabited continent on earth

Early Settlers in the Deserts and Savannahs

Australia's deserts hindered the expansion of settlement. European explorers reported that there was not enough water in them to allow towns and villages to flourish. Cattle could be grazed in the semi-arid savannahs, but attempts at settlement often failed. Australia's deserts are scattered with the remains of buildings that have been abandoned as settlers left, unable to prosper in the extreme conditions and isolation.

Deserts made travel and communication between the colonies difficult. People could not easily cross a desert and had to either take a very long route around them or travel on ships along the coast to reach other towns and settlements.

The scattered settlement in the deserts and savannahs resulted in these areas being one of the most untouched environments in Australia. However, feral animals, mining, tourism and defence force activities have now caused changes to parts of the desert ecosystems.

Overland Telegraph Line

The Overland Telegraph Line was laid through the desert from Adelaide to Darwin in 1872. The international telegraph cable linking Australia to Britain came ashore at Darwin. People in the main centres of population in the south of Australia needed to find a way across the deserts so that a telegraph line could be laid to connect Australia to the rest of the world. The laying of the Overland Telegraph Line was one of the 19th century's most remarkable engineering achievements.

Afghan Cameleers

Afghan cameleers provided a transport service and the supply of goods to settlers across the deserts during the 1800s. The Afghans accompanied many of the explorers, who could not have succeeded without their assistance.

In 1873, William Gosse became the first European to see and climb Uluru, which he named Ayers Rock. Kamran, an Afghan cameleer, accompanied Gosse. In his journal, Gosse wrote,

> *"How I envied Kamran his hard feet; he seemed to enjoy the walking about with bare feet, while mine were all in blisters."*

Health And Education

The Royal Flying Doctor Service provides people living in remote desert regions with access to doctors, nurses and dentists.

The School of the Air allows outback children to keep up with their education. The first lessons were broadcast by radio from Alice Springs in the 1940s. Children and their teachers could speak to each other over a radio system using electricity that was generated by pedals. Today, technology such as webcams and computers make it easier for students to interact with each other and the teachers.

FAST FACTS

Large towns in the deserts of Australia:

Kalgoorlie
Alice Springs
Mount Isa
Broken Hill

Water in Australian Deserts

Although Australia's deserts are dry, sandy places, they still have some sources of water.

Water Cycle and the Desert

In temperate regions, the water cycle brings rain to the land. In Australia's deserts, rain rarely falls. Any water that evaporates is carried away to other areas. When this moisture in the air reaches a region of cold air, water condenses forming clouds and rain. This rain falls into the ocean or onto land, where rivers carry it back into the desert. The cycle then starts again as the water in the desert evaporates in the intense heat.

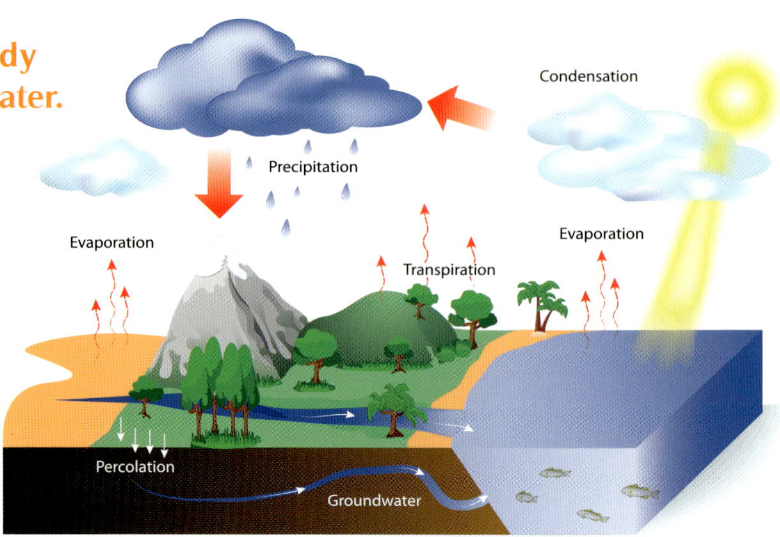

Underground Water

Some water exists in underground reserves and comes to the surface as springs. Over time, mineral deposits in the water can cause a mound to build up around the spring. These mound springs were very important for the traditional Aboriginal lifestyle, wildlife and livestock. Water from the mound flows around it creating a pool, which can be a permanent oasis in the desert. The Dalhousie Springs are a large and well-known mound spring in the Australian desert.

The Great Artesian Basin is a freshwater source that lies underneath more than 20 per cent of Australia, much of it beneath desert areas. This underground water is a mixture of ancient freshwater as well as top-up water that seeps into it from areas where there is high rainfall, such as along the Great Dividing Range.

The Great Artesian Basin is under threat from overuse and water flows have declined since people began drawing from it for livestock and mining.

Below: Dalhousie Springs

Rain

Deserts can experience floods when sudden thunderstorms fill shallow depressions in the land. These quickly dry up but plants and animals make use of them while they can.

Above: Flooded outback Central Australia

Rivers and Creeks

When heavy rain falls in areas outside the deserts, water flows along rivers and creeks that are normally dry, eventually providing water to arid regions. The monsoon in northern Australia sends water into the inland deserts in this way. Many desert plants and animals have developed adaptations to take advantage of these temporary sources of water, which quickly dry up.

Salt Lakes

Salt lakes exist throughout Australia's deserts. They are low-lying areas into which creeks drain when there is rain. The extreme heat evaporates all the water leaving only a salty covering on the dry lakebed. When there is water in these lakes, birds migrate to them from other areas, fish and frogs appear, and plants bloom quickly, producing large quantities of seeds. Budgerigars fly for long distances to feed on the seeds produced by desert plants after rain. Shrimps and fish produce eggs, which can survive long periods buried in the desert until rain comes again. They then grow very quickly so that they can breed before the water dries up.

Kati Thanda - Lake Eyre in South Australia is a salt lake that periodically becomes the largest freshwater lake in Australia when it fills with water.

Ord River Irrigation Scheme

This massive irrigation scheme in the north of Western Australia involved damming the Ord River. Lake Argyle was produced as a result and it is now one of the largest artificial lakes in the world, holding more water than Sydney Harbour.

Deserts and the Australian Economy

Tourism

Australia's deserts attract people who want to experience the open spaces and the bright night skies, unaffected by the lights of a city. Many desert locations are on traditional Aboriginal land. Tourists may need to obtain permits to visit them and respect should be shown towards areas of spiritual significance.

Mining

Mining in the deserts provides employment and contributes to the Australian economy. The fragile ecosystems in the desert can be easily destroyed and there needs to be a balance between preserving the habitat for plants and animals, and using mined resources for economic benefit.

Above: Woomera Missile Park

Defence Force Areas

Australia's desert areas are the sites of a number of military and security facilities.

Maralinga, SA
the site of atomic bomb tests from 1955 to 1963
Woomera Prohibited Area, SA
a rocket testing establishment
Defence Facility Pine Gap, NT
a satellite tracking and communications centre

Using Feral Animals

- Camels are exported to Saudi Arabia, mainly for meat.
- Rabbits were once widely sold locally for meat.
- Wild horses can be caught and tamed.
- Recreational shooters hunt wild pigs.

Art

Art in Australia often looks to the deserts for inspiration. Famous artists such as Russell Drysdale, Albert Namatjira and Sidney Nolan used the desert landscapes in their paintings. The Papunya Tula art of the Aboriginal desert painters is sought by art collectors around Australia and the world.

Cattle Industry

Australia has a thriving beef cattle industry in the savannahs. Although the restricted water supply and the saltbush that the cattle eat both make the savannahs unsuitable for raising dairy cattle, farmers successfully raise beef cattle. They make up for the sparse feed by having extremely large areas on which the cattle can graze.

Early settlers who drove their cattle into the savannahs to graze believed that the hot, dry conditions would result in fewer tick infestations than in wetter climates. They later introduced cattle breeds, such as the Brahman, that can tolerate semi-arid areas.

Canning Stock Route

The Canning Stock Route is one of the longest stock routes in the world, covering 1,800 kilometres across the desert in Western Australia. It crosses the Gibson Desert, the Little Sandy Desert and the Great Sandy Desert. Alfred Canning first surveyed it in 1906, and his aim was to provide a route for droving cattle from the Kimberley region in the north down to Kalgoorlie where they would be sold.

The provision of water along the route was the most important resource that Canning was looking for. He relied on the water sources that Aboriginal people had been using for thousands of years, but this resulted in incidents of violent conflict and the ruination of many of the water holes.

The Canning Stock Route was never very successful and the land it traverses is now largely back in the hands of its traditional Aboriginal owners. It is now also a tourist route used by visitors who want to see the deserts of Australia for themselves.

Below: Windy Corner on the Canning Stock Route

Australian Deserts and Environmental Sustainability

Food Webs And Threatened Species

Deserts are places of extreme climatic conditions, with finely balanced ecosystems. A change in any part of the desert food web can quickly result in the extinction of species that cannot relocate.

The food web in the desert has grasses, bushes, seeds and fruits at its base. Overgrazing by feral animals can drive this vegetation to the brink of extinction.

The next level of the food web includes all the insects, birds and mammals that eat the desert plants. If the vegetation dies or is overgrazed, these animals also disappear.

The top level of the food web includes the predators that eat the smaller creatures. The main desert predators are the large lizards and snakes, dingoes and eagles. These creatures have the advantage of being able to migrate away from areas if the smaller animal population decreases.

UNESCO World Heritage Sites in Australia's arid regions

- Purnululu National Park WA - the site of the Bungle Bungle rocks
- Willandra Lakes Region NSW - the source of archaeological finds about the earliest history of humanity
- Uluru-Kata Tjuta National Park NT
- Australian Fossil Mammal Site Riversleigh QLD

Feral Animals

The feral animals in Australia's deserts are descended from domesticated animals that have either escaped or been released into the wild. They include camels, horses, donkeys, wild pigs, goats, cats, dogs and rabbits. These animals are all very destructive. They ruin water holes, overgraze and kill small animals. They provide no environmental contribution to the natural desert ecology.

Biodiversity

Threats to the biodiversity of the Australian deserts include:

- Muddying and pollution of water sources
- Climate change
- Mining, tourism and the grazing of livestock
- Weeds and feral animals

Plants and Animals in Australia's Deserts

How Native Plants Survive in the Deserts

mallee trees
Having underground tubers that keep the plant alive even if the leaves are burned or dry out

native daisies
Growing quickly after rain and producing seeds that wait for the next rainfall before they sprout

saltbush
Having silvery leaves that reflect light and therefore keep the plant cool

spinifex grass
Having roots that grow a long way down into the ground

How Native Animals Survive in the Deserts

water birds
Migrating away when water dries up and only moving back into the desert after rain

kangaroos, dingoes
Resting under bushes or in caves during the day

mammals, birds
Having light coloured fur and feathers that reflect heat

lizards, small mammls
Being active at night and sheltering from the heat during the day

lizards, snakes
Hiding in cracks in rocks or under clumps of spinifex during the day

thorny devil lizards, some insects
Collecting dew on their own bodies and then drinking it

some frogs, bilbies, perenties
Burrowing deep under the ground

kangaroos, dingoes, emus
Making use of man-made waterholes

hopping mouse
Producing dry droppings to conserve body water

bilbies
Having large ears that allow body heat to be lost

kangaroos
Licking fur so that the evaporation of the moisture will cool them

HOW DO FERAL CAMELS SURVIVE IN THE DESERT?

- They can close their nostrils against the sand storms
- Their spreading soft feet can walk easily on sand
- They can drink water with a high salt content
- They can survive for long periods without drinking
- They produce dry droppings

Australia's Largest Deserts

1. Great Victoria Desert

Location

The Great Victoria Desert is in the south of Western Australia and extends into South Australia.

Description

The Great Victoria Desert is the largest desert in Australia. It includes stony gibber plains, salt lakes and red sand hills. It was named in 1875 by Ernest Giles, the first European to cross this desert.

Traditional Owners

The traditional owners of the Great Victoria Desert are the Maralinga Tjarutja people.

FAST FACT

The Woomera Prohibited Area is in the Great Victoria Desert. It is a military testing site that supports Australia's national security.

Desert Animals and Plants

- Princess parrot
- Major Mitchell cockatoo
- Mallee fowl
- Woma python
- Southern marsupial mole
- Gould's goanna
- Australian bustard
- Scarlet-chested parrot
- Spinifex
- Saltbush

Economic Activities in the Great Victoria Desert

- **Tourism**
  Visitors to the Great Victoria Desert must obtain permits to enter some areas. There are no facilities so all fuel, food and water have to be carried.

- **Mining**
  Surface mining for gold occurs on the edge of the desert, and there are reserves of iron ore and other minerals, which have not been mined. The Great Victoria Desert Biodiversity Trust was set up under the mining requirements established by the Western Australian government. The Trust's role is to investigate conservation and biodiversity in relation to mining activities.

- **Livestock Grazing**
  There has never been large scale grazing of livestock in the Great Victoria Desert. Because of this there are very few weeds to compete with native vegetation.

NUCLEAR TESTING

Nuclear weapons were tested at Maralinga in the 1950s. Some Aboriginal people were exposed to nuclear fallout and the effects of contamination of the environment.

Princess parrot

Major Mitchell cockatoo

Gould's goanna

Australian bustard

Saltbush

2. Great Sandy Desert

Location

The Great Sandy Desert is in the north of Western Australia and extends into a part of the Northern Territory. Its western limit is the Indian Ocean at Eighty Mile Beach on the Western Australian coast.

Description

The Great Sandy Desert includes stony gibber plains, salt lakes and red sand dunes. There are also regions of savannah grassland with a few gum trees. The first European explorer to cross the Great Sandy Desert was Peter Warburton in 1874. An Aboriginal man named Charley assisted him. Warburton claimed that he would have died if Charley had not helped him.

The two main population centres are at Telfer, a mining town, and Yulara, which is the service centre for the Uluru-Kata Tjuta National Park. The Wolfe Creek meteorite crater is in the north of this desert. The crater is 300,000 years old and the meteorite that fell there weighed about 50,000 tonnes. The Djaru people call the crater Kandimalal.

Traditional Owners

The Martu and Pintupi people are the traditional owners of the Great Sandy Desert. A Martu couple, Warri and Yatungka, may have been the last Australian Aboriginal people who had never come into contact with Europeans. When they came out of the desert in 1974, their story was reported across Australia and created widespread interest.

Desert Animals and Plants

- Marsupial mole
- Rufous hare-wallaby
- Bilby
- Spinifex

Economic Activities in the Great Sandy Desert

- **Tourism**
  Uluru-Kata Tjuta National Park is in the south east of this desert. The tourist facilities are confined as much as possible to specific areas. People travelling through the desert are asked to keep to the tracks to avoid damaging the environment.

- **Mining**
  Gold and copper have been mined in this desert and there are uranium reserves, which have not yet been touched.

- **Livestock Grazing**
  Cattle are grazed in the western part of this desert on about 7 per cent of the total desert area.

- **The Arts**
  The Aboriginal people of this desert have developed a thriving art movement.

FAST FACT
Deserts and semi-arid savannahs make up 70% of Australia.
Marsupial mole
Rufous Hare-wallaby
Bilby
Spinifex

3. Tanami Desert

Location

The Tanami Desert stretches from the Kimberley region in Western Australia to near Alice Springs in the Northern Territory.

Description

The Tanami Desert has mostly flat, red sand plains.

Traditional Owners

The Kukatja and Warlpiri people are the traditional owners of the Tanami Desert. The main townships in the Tanami Desert are the communities of Yuendumu, Nyirrpi, Willowra and Lajamanu.

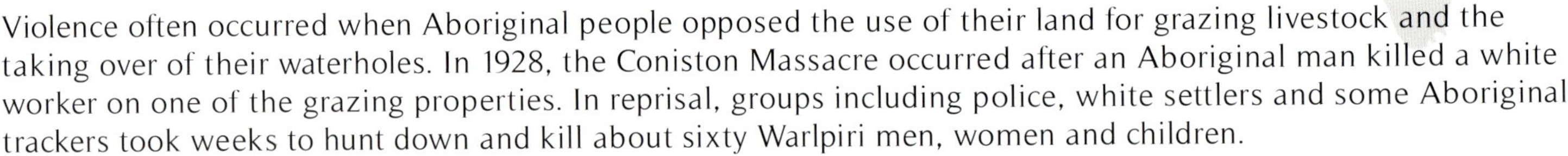

Violence often occurred when Aboriginal people opposed the use of their land for grazing livestock and the taking over of their waterholes. In 1928, the Coniston Massacre occurred after an Aboriginal man killed a white worker on one of the grazing properties. In reprisal, groups including police, white settlers and some Aboriginal trackers took weeks to hunt down and kill about sixty Warlpiri men, women and children.

Economic Activities in the Tanami Desert

- **Tourism**
  The Tanami Track crosses this desert and gives tourists a route they can follow to see its isolated beauty. Unlike the larger deserts in Australia, the Tanami does have some tourist stops where limited facilities and fuel are available. The Stuart Highway also crosses parts of the Tanami Desert.

- **Mining**
  Gold is mined in underground operations in the Tanami Desert. The mining operators monitor water quality, noise, dust emissions and the presence in the environment of cyanide, which is used to extract gold from the ore.

- **Livestock Grazing**
  There are a few pastoral areas in the Tanami Desert. The lack of water has kept 75 per cent of the Tanami Desert free from the effects of livestock on the natural ecosystem.

Desert Animals and Plants

- Western chestnut mouse
- Little native mouse
- Long-tailed planigale
- Grey falcon
- Australian painted snipe
- Freckled duck
- Western hare-wallaby
- Spinifex
- Native rock fig

Western chestnut mouse Grey falcon Australian painted snipe Freckled duck

Karlu Karlu / Devils Marbles

Located on the Stuart Highway on the edge of the Tanami Desert, these rock formations have been formed by erosion. They are only the tip of a large mass of granite rock that is beneath the ground. The Karlu Karlu are a sacred site for the Kaytete, Warumungu, Warlpiri and Alyawarra traditional owners. Visitors are therefore asked not to climb the rocks. Animals around the Karlu Karlu include Fairy Martins, little birds that build mud nests hanging from the undersides of the boulders. This keeps their nestlings in the shade. There are also finches, black-headed goannas and large sand goannas that live in the microclimates created in the desert by the huge, balancing boulders.

Newhaven Wildlife Sanctuary

The Newhaven Wildlife Sanctuary is one of Australia's largest non-government areas for the protection of wildlife. It is a bird-watching destination that is home to 170 species of birds. The Sanctuary covers 262,000 hectares and involves the Warlpiri people in its management.

4. Simpson Desert

Location

The Simpson Desert is located across three states. They are South Australia, Queensland and the Northern Territory.

Description

The Simpson Desert has parallel, red sand dunes that cover hundreds of kilometres. These dunes do not move, as in some deserts, but are mostly held in place by vegetation. Salt lakes and grass plains are also found in the Simpson Desert. The summertime temperatures can be extreme, exceeding 50°C, and South Australian National Parks authorities close the area to tourists during these times. Park passes are required before entering the Simpson Desert Conservation Park or Simpson Desert Regional Reserve. No pets can be taken into the park since feral animals are one of the threats to the desert's ecosystems. Apart from the few permanent water holes, the desert also receives a small amount of rain that causes the plant life to have sudden and brief explosions of growth. The Great Artesian Basin lies under the Simpson Desert. Although the surface is dry, there is a large source of underground water, which comes to the surface as springs or from bores.

The first European to see the Simpson Desert was Charles Sturt in 1845.

Kestrel | Zebra finch | Perentie | Poached-egg daisies | Grevillea

Traditional Owners

Wangkangurru, Yarliyandi and Arrernte people are the traditional owners of the Simpson Desert. Passing on knowledge of the location of water holes was always vital to their existence. This knowledge was transferred in art and ceremonies. They actively dug and maintained the springs over generations, and these water sources kept the people alive as they travelled throughout their country in search of food. Pastoralists were desperate to find the locations of these wells, sometimes using force to make Aboriginal people tell them where they were.

Desert Animals and Plants

- Water-holding frog
- Wedge-tailed eagle
- Kestrel
- Crested pigeon
- Zebra finch
- Galah
- Corellas
- Perentie
- Spinifex
- Poached-egg daisies
- Grevilleas
- Acacias
- Samphire

Economic Activities in the Simpson Desert

- **Mining**
  A gas pipeline runs across the Simpson Desert, but there is no large-scale mining.

- **Livestock Grazing**
  Cattle grazing occurs on the edges of the desert region.

FAST FACT

The tallest sand dune in the Simpson Desert is called Nappanerica or Big Red. It is 40 metres high.

Kati Thanda-Lake Eyre

Kati Thanda-Lake Eyre is Australia's largest salt lake. It periodically fills with water, which then evaporates to leave a salty crust. The extent of water in the lake depends on the monsoon in the areas that are the sources of the rivers that flow into it. As the lake fills, thousands of waterbirds migrate to it. They include birds that are normally only seen in seaside locations, such as pelicans, gulls and terns. The birds feed on insects and on the small fish that multiply in the lake.

Dalhousie Springs

These hot, mineral springs rise naturally from the Great Artesian Basin. The springs are an oasis in the desert and support unique species of fish that have evolved there in complete isolation.

5. Gibson Desert

Location

The Gibson Desert is in central Western Australia.

Description

The Gibson Desert has sand dunes, gibber plains and some small salt lakes. In 1876, Ernest Giles became the first European to cross the Gibson Desert. He named it after one of his team who died on the journey. Despite the extreme dryness of this desert, there is underground water in the Officer Basin and Canning Basin. Lake Gruszka near Warbuton is a surprisingly large lake in the Gibson Desert. It is surrounded with vegetation and attracts ducks and other waterbirds.

Mulgara | Marsupial mole | Ghost bat | Black-footed rock wallaby | Greater bilby

Traditional Owners

The largest communities in the Gibson Desert are at Kanpa, Patjarr, Kaltukatjara, Kintore and Tjirrkarli. Warburton at the southern edge of the desert has its own airstrip. The Pintupi people are the traditional owners and they have a town centre at Patjarr, run by the Ngaanyatjarra Council. The Pintupi were moved out of the Gibson Desert during the 1960s, when the area was used by the Australian government for weapons testing. After the Pintupi people were removed, their desert homelands were declared a Nature Reserve, which prohibited them from returning and living there. The Pintupi people have now returned to their traditional lands despite this prohibition.

Endangered Animals in the Gibson Desert

- Mulgara (related to the Tasmanian Devil but only 20 cm long)
- Marsupial mole
- Ghost bat
- Black-footed rock wallaby
- Greater bilby

Economic Activities in the Gibson Desert

- **Mining**
  There are reserves of copper, gold and diamonds in the Gibson Desert.

- **Livestock Grazing**
  Since there are no sources of water suitable for cattle, there is no stock grazing within the Gibson Desert. Despite this, feral camels have increased in numbers in recent years and are a threat to the natural ecosystems. Camels graze on the desert vegetation and therefore contribute to erosion as the plants they eat die and no longer hold the sand and soil in place.

- **Sandalwood**
  The Ngaanyatjarra Council is considering the possibility of making economic use of sandalwood trees in the area.

6. Little Sandy Desert

Location

The Little Sandy Desert is in the centre of Western Australia in the East Pilbara region. It is part of the Rudall River National Park.

Description

The Little Sandy Desert has sand dunes and low, rocky hills. The Rudall River, or Karlamilyi, flows through the desert and there are wetlands along its course. It drains into Lake Dora, which becomes a salt lake when its waters dry up. The rocky hills have some permanent water sources, and there are also man-made water holes left after the creation of the Canning Stock Route. The town of Jigalong is on the edge of the desert. Its population is about 400 people, mostly Aboriginal Australians.

Traditional Owners

The traditional owners of the Little Sandy Desert are the Mandilara people. Parnngurr and Punmu are two of the Aboriginal communities. The caves and rock walls in the hills of this desert are well known for their Aboriginal rock art.

Desert Animals

There is a great variety of lizards in the Little Sandy Desert, probably due to the perfect habitat for them amongst the rocky hills. Unfortunately, camels are responsible for damaging many of the water sources. Recent studies show an increase in feral cats and a decrease in bilbies and mulgara.

Economic Activities in the Little Sandy Desert

- **Tourism**

  There are no facilities for tourists in the Little Sandy Desert, and it is a harsh and dangerous place for anyone not used to living there. Although water is not easy to find, there can be sudden, dangerous floods.

- **Mining**

  Mineral exploration is an important economic activity close to this desert. This includes copper and gold mining and uranium exploration. The building of access roads has effects on the desert but the mines also provide employment and contribute to Australia's economy. The professional mining workforce generally does not live in the desert but flies in for work.

- **Livestock Grazing**

  Livestock are grazed in a very small portion in the east of this desert, since there are no water sources suitable for sustaining large-scale grazing of animals. The lack of grazing also means that introduced weeds are not a problem to the environment.

7. Strzelecki Desert

Location

The Strzelecki Desert is located across parts of South Australia, Queensland and New South Wales.

Description

The Strzelecki Desert features sand dunes and salt lakes. Charles Sturt named it after the Polish explorer, Paul Strzelecki. The Strzelecki Creek, Cooper Creek and the Diamantina River all run through this desert. They are often dry but may fill suddenly after rain. The Strzelecki Regional Reserve protects part of this desert.

Brolga Dunnart Sandy inland mouse Long-haired rat River red gum

Desert Animals and Plants

- Dusky hopping-mouse
- Brolga
- Mulgara
- Dunnart
- Sandy inland mouse
- Long-haired rat
- River red gum

Economic Activities in the Strzelecki Desert

- **Tourism**

  Tourists visit the area to enjoy four-wheel drive camping trips and a desert experience. The Birdsville Track passes through the Strzelecki Desert.

- **Mining**

  The Strzelecki Track is used for mining access. The Moomba oil and gas processing plant and the associated mining operations are important industrial developments in the Strzelecki Desert. Moomba uses bore water and it has its own large airstrip.

- **Livestock Grazing**

  There is extensive livestock grazing in the Strzelecki Desert. An increase in the number of goats grazing is contributing to damage of the desert vegetation since goats can get into areas that are inaccessible for larger grazing animals.

8. Sturt Stony Desert

Location
The Sturt Stony Desert is located in the northeast of South Australia and in neighbouring parts of Queensland and New South Wales.

Description
The Sturt Stony Desert is a gibber desert, meaning it is covered in stones. The stones are glazed with a natural covering of iron oxide, which gives them a purple-reddish colour. The explorer Charles Sturt and his team took their horses into this desert and found the stones very damaging to the horses' hooves and legs. A number of creeks drain into this desert, but they are mostly dry except after rain.

Traditional Owners
The traditional owners of the Sturt Stony Desert are the Dieri, the Yandruwantha, the Yawarawarrka and the Ngamini. These people made use of the hard stones in this gibber desert to make tools and weapons.

There were numerous massacres of Aboriginal people by white settlers in this area. In the 1880s, the Warrhampa massacre occurred at the Goyder Lagoon when cattle owners killed many Aboriginal people.

Desert Animals and Plants
- Kowari
- Saltbush
- Grevillea

Kowari Saltbush Grevillia

Economic Activities in the Sturt Stony Desert
- **Tourism**
  The Diamantina Road and the Birdsville Track cross this desert and provide tourists with access to remote areas.

- **Mining**
  There are gas and oil fields on the edges of the desert.

- **Livestock Grazing**
  Some parts of this desert are grazed, and cattle use the underground bore water. Despite the seeming lack of feed, the Sturt Stony Desert manages to support a few cattle stations, as well as kangaroos and a variety of smaller animals.

9. Tirari Desert

Location
The Tirari Desert is in South Australia.

Description
The features of the Tirari Desert are its sand dunes and salt lakes. Cooper Creek crosses this desert but the creek bed is often dry, except after rain. Part of the desert is in the Kati Thanda-Lake Eyre National Park. The first European explorer was Peter Warburton in 1866.

Traditional Owners
The Dieri people of the Tirari Desert may have numbered about 1,000 in the mid 1800s. The Dieri Native Title Claim extends along the eastern edge of Kati Thanda-Lake Eyre.

The Dieri language was studied and recorded in detail by German Lutheran missionaries who worked in the area in 1869. They ran a school for the Aboriginal children where the Dieri language was spoken and written. The remains of this Killalpaninna Mission are a South Australian heritage site.

Economic Activities in the Tirari Desert

- **Tourism**
  The Tirari Desert is only visited by a small number of tourists. There are no facilities for camping and visitors need to be very experienced in survival in remote, arid areas.

- **Livestock Grazing**
  There are large cattle stations in the Tirari Desert. They use underground water sources.

Desert Animals and Plants
Fossil remains of ancient types of ringtail possums in the Tirari Desert suggest that the area was once much wetter, with forest trees.

The plants of the Tirari Desert are mostly low wattle bushes, saltbush and grasses. After rain, small shrubs and flowering plants bloom abundantly. The red river gum and coolabah trees grow around permanent water holes and springs.

10. Pedirka Desert

Location

The Pedirka Desert is in South Australia. The closest sizeable town is Oodnadatta and the northern border of this desert is the Hamilton Creek.

Description

The Pedirka Desert is a stony or gibber desert, like the Gibson Desert and Sturt Stony Desert, but much smaller. It also has low, red sand dunes.

Desert Animals and Plants

The vegetation of the Pedirka Desert is mostly mulga scrub, with grasses and saltbush. Near the Hamilton River, red river gums and coolabah trees take advantage of the water. As with all the deserts in Australia, there is a short-lived bloom of flowering plants after rain.

Pedirka Railway Station Ruins, Oodnadatta Track

Economic Activities in the Pedirka Desert

- **Mining**

  Petroleum, natural gas and coal exploration have occurred in the region of the Pedirka Desert, but the lack of bore water over the central part of the desert has limited the possibilities for any economic activity there.

  The Rumbulara Ochre Mine operated during the Second World War, producing pigments to use in camouflage. The mine once had its own railway siding. There was no local water so it had to be brought on the train and then by truck to the mine site. The mine employed ten Aboriginal miners.

  The ochre mine was used by Aboriginal people for generations before its European owners started mining there. A government report from 1944 states:

> *"The existence of the ochre deposits in this locality was known to the natives before the corning of the white man. It is believed that the material was highly prized among them for the decoration of their bodies. It was of special importance for ceremonial occasions and was traded over long distances. Natives still visit the locality and take away a few pounds of the ochre."*

- **Livestock Grazing**

  A large part of this desert is used for cattle grazing. Groundwater for cattle is accessed along the western part of the desert.

- **Railway**

  During the building of The Ghan Railway, there was a small side track called Pedirka. This was used to load building materials and supplies.

Nullarbor Plain

The Nullarbor Plain is the world's largest expanse of exposed limestone, covering 200,000 square kilometres. Although it is the third largest arid area in Australia, the Nullarbor Plain is called a karst and not a desert. A karst is an area of land that sits on a base of limestone. The Nullarbor Plain was once a seabed and the remains of ancient sea life form its rocks. Weathering of the limestone by water has produced a system of underground caves, many with large pools of hidden fresh water.

The Nullarbor Plain stretches from South Australia to Western Australia and meets the Southern Ocean along the Great Australian Bight. The Bunda Cliffs rise steeply from the ocean below, revealing layers of exposed limestone.

Nullarbor means 'treeless' in Latin. The dryness on the surface and the poor soil can only support saltbush and grasses. In some parts, there are pockets of mulga trees. The driest parts of the Nullarbor Plain have no creeks or rivers, and any rain that does fall seeps into the limestone below.

Human Use of the Nullarbor Plain

Explorers

Edward John Eyre explored the Great Australian Bight and the Nullarbor Plain in 1840 and 1841.

The Eyre Highway

The Eyre Highway crosses the Nullarbor Plain and is the main road route connecting South Australia and Western Australia. Campsites and businesses offering food, accommodation and fuel cater for truck drivers and tourists.

Livestock Grazing

The outer edges of the Nullarbor Plain are used for livestock grazing. Across the centre of the plain, the lack of bore water restricts all human activity and settlement.

Railway

The Indian Pacific railway crosses the Nullarbor Plain. Construction of the tracks started at opposite ends of the continent and met in the middle in 1917. The railway builders made use of Ooldea's natural permanent water supply, a rarity in the Nullarbor and a site of importance to the Aboriginal inhabitants.

Quarantine

There are restrictions on bringing some plants and animals into both South Australia and Western Australia and travellers have to pass quarantine checkpoints at both ends of a trip across the Nullarbor Plain.

Overland Telegraph

The remains of an old telegraph station at Eucla are a reminder of the time when the Overland Telegraph Line was a vital means of communication. Sand has now buried parts of the building. Eucla was established in 1877, and once had its own jetty and rail line.

Australian Aboriginal People and the Nullarbor Plain

Australian Aboriginal people have a long history of living on the Nullarbor Plain, and of making use of its resources.

Koonalda Cave and Allen's Cave

Archaeologists believe that people occupied the Koonalda Cave 24,000 years ago. The cave was an underground flint mine where quarrying must have required burning torches for light. The hard pieces of flint were needed for making the tips of tools and weapons. Seventy metres below ground level, archaeologists have found the ancient remains of a fireplace. There are also rock walls covered with a crisscross pattern of finger markings. At Allen's Cave, near the town of Eucla, the signs of human activity are even older, dating back to possibly 40,000 years ago.

USING MAPS

Search Google Maps or Google Earth for a satellite view of the Nullarbor Plain, which is clearly visible. Why is the colour of the Nullarbor Plain different from the areas surrounding it?

Glossary

biodiversity	the range of living things in an area
condensation	the change from a gaseous state into a liquid state
evaporation	the change from a liquid state into a gaseous state
gibber	desert covered in stones
iconic	being famous as a symbol for something
migration	mass movement of animals over long distances
parallel	positioned in straight lines in the same direction
tuber	thick plant root

Index

Afghan cameleers 8
Canning Stock Route 13,25
Coniston Massacre 20
explorers 4,8,18,26-28,30
food web 14
Great Artesian Basin 10,22,23
Karlu Karlu 21
Kati Thanda - Lake Eyre 11,23,28
ochre mine 29
Ord River Irrigation Scheme 11
Overland Telegraph Line 8,30
School of the Air 8
Uluru - Kata Tjuta 8,14,18
Wolfe Creek Crater 18
World Heritage Sites 14

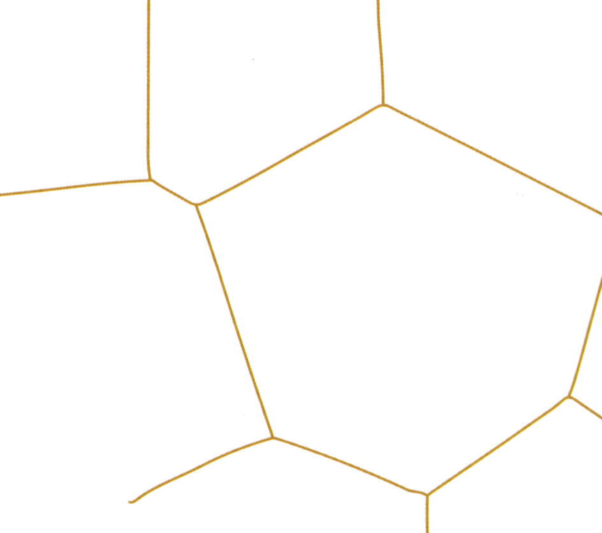

Visit this website to find out more about Australia's deserts:
www.australia.gov.au/about-australia/our-country
(Hint: type the word 'deserts' into the search box on this website)